Walking with the Wind

Poems by Abbas Kiarostami

تقدیم به دوست گرامی من
فضل الله زهرائی
که از دست ایشان و مهربانی ایشان
کتابهای فراوان اینجا رسید

with best wishes

مترجم دوّم
مایکل برد — MCB

Walking with the Wind

Poems by Abbas Kiarostami

BILINGUAL EDITION

Translated from the Persian by Ahmad Karimi-Hakkak and Michael Beard

A HARVARD FILM ARCHIVE PUBLICATION CAMBRIDGE, MASSACHUSETTS, AND LONDON, ENGLAND ~ 2001

DISTRIBUTED BY HARVARD UNIVERSITY PRESS

INTRODUCTION

Ahmad Karimi-Hakkak and Michael Beard

It is easy to believe that the Abbas Kiarostami who wrote this volume of poetry is the same Kiarostami who has created such extraordinary films as *Close-Up* and *Taste of Cherry;* it is harder to place the artist within his native aesthetic tradition. The cinematic moments in *Walking with the Wind* are what we notice first. At times the vignettes it contains recall the camera shots in his films that last just long enough to establish our identification before moving on. At times there is a complex interplay between points of view, established so quickly that our impulse is to reach for the pause button. One of the building blocks of Kiarostami's films, a scene in which two characters see themselves differently, is depicted in the poem on page 44. Here, three vantage points, each emerging naturally, are expressed in such a nonchalant way that the presentation belies the poem's complexity:

How merciful
that the turtle doesn't see
the little bird's effortless flight.

The three vantage points—turtle's, bird's, human observer's (or camera's)—may leave us wondering where we stand, both literally and metaphorically. Somewhere beyond the three viewpoints (ours as well as theirs) we sense a vision that lights the flame of an impossible desire.

The preface to the Persian edition of these poems compares them to flashes of lightning between stretches of darkness. We like the image not so much for its grandeur or magnificence but for its speed. The illumination cast by these poems manifests itself suddenly, and the subjects are in constant motion. A collection of Japanese haiku, which in some ways *Walking with the Wind* resembles, may meander from one vignette to another, but rarely with the same feeling of restlessness and acceleration.

And yet even a restless eye can observe closely. These poems are deliberate and gradual enough to present lessons in how to perceive nuances. Take the opening poem. If we read it against the backdrop of the contrasting opposites that create the struts and beams of classical Persian poetry, the comparison makes us aware of more delicate shades:

A white foal
emerges through the fog
and disappears
in the fog.

At first the poem may seem to privilege a contrast between black and white. In the end we find ourselves faced with subtler distinctions. The poem alerts us that we will be shown a world of slight differences. Or, consider the poem on page 98:

> *Snow descends*
> *from the black clouds*
> *with the whiteness of snow.*

The reiterated whiteness seems to make it necessary to compare the snow to itself.

Even when the poems shift, careen, and slide subtly from one scene to the next—presenting images in motion, like the horse in the opening poem, alerting us to a world in which things will show up briefly and disappear, or the snow in the next, or the clouds a few poems later—the glimpse is in sharp focus. Although the scenes themselves may elude us—the footprints in snow in the poem on page 19, the pigeon three poems later, or the various animals and passersby whose motives, habits, and trajectories extend outside the frame—the elusive can also be exact.

The aesthetic of close observation is akin to the aesthetic of familiar objects: the imperative to pause and look more closely at daily experience. And yet it is not necessarily Kiarostami's cinematic instincts that we experience in these poems. Film celebrates the specific landscape—and this may be eminently true of Kiarostami's filmmaking, where the layout of a village, the landscape of the abrasive and irregular or textured and grainy, take precedence over the expected or the generic. Language, without the resources of detail allowed by the camera, can rarely achieve the same visual density. The poems of *Walking with the Wind* don't even seem to evoke particular landscapes. There are poems here in which the act of perception can be the whole point, as in the poem on page 57:

Autumn afternoon:
a sycamore leaf
falls softly
and rests
on its own shadow.

Strictly speaking, it is obvious that a leaf falls on its shadow. It is a process so logical it should bear no comment, except, of course, that the observer can forget the logical conclusion that shadow and leaf are connected. Observation corrects consciousness. It is our unscientific selves who are capable of surprise at how exactly the two match up.

Where does Kiarostami's leaf fall in relation to the long and imposing shadow of Persian poetry? Stylistically, no poet in the last half century or so has gone as far as Kiarostami to signal a break with the formal features of poetry in that glorious, millennium-old aesthetic tradition. Even Nima Yushij (1897–1960), the poet most often cited as the modernizer of Persian poetry, did not break entirely free of rhyme and meter. In that sense, at least, Kiarostami may be called the most radical Iranian poet of his generation, perhaps of the century. Thematically, Kiarostami the poet relies more substantively on the conventions that define poetry in his culture. He certainly uses the basic conceptual elements of the Persian lyrical tradition, often with philosophical or meditative underpinnings. The technique of developing poetic discourse through pairs of corresponding or oppositional images, concepts, or modes of existence informs both the ghazals of Rumi (1207–73) and Hafez (1320–88) and shapes a great number of the poems in this volume. Thus the white of snow, while it contrasts with the color of coal or of the raven's wings, coincides aesthetically with the white of the pigeon or the cloud.

This play of correspondences and contrasts—of age and youth or of smooth surfaces versus craggy ones—appears more stark in those compositions, like the poem on page 69, that simply record observations without explicitly or implicitly commenting upon them:

An old villager
on the mountain path —
a young man's call from afar.

Or the poem on page 74, where the contrast between the moon and the mountain peak generates a mood of buoyancy and escape:

The round moon
rises gingerly
above the volcanic peak.

At times, the principle of contrasts turns into a transformative power that stretches from the observed scene to the desire within the poem. The contrast between the roaring train and the butterfly sleeping on the rail, and the halting of one before the other in the poem on page 167, conveys not just an observed event but a colossal will to change the way of the world. Similarly, the visible correspondence and conceptual opposition between the crescent "new" moon and the "worn-out" sickles on page 192, a direct borrowing from Hafez, the greatest Persian lyricist of all, opens a conceptual space far beyond the image at hand. In a famous poem by Hafez, the crescent "blade" of the new moon against the backdrop of the blue-green evening sky calls the speaker inward to regret how little he has cultivated, how little he can expect to reap at harvest time. Kiarostami's variation makes the pale moon seem to overpower the emblems of physical work.

There is something in the scope of our poet's project that resembles another tradition of Persian aesthetics. Like Rumi, the poet of the largest questions in all of Persian poetry, he reaches out to the world rather than focusing on any local topic. His thinking is cosmopolitan, humane, and global. This may explain the simultaneous presence of the nun, the soldier, the villager, and the many other characters that populate these poems. The simplest classification would include humans and animals; but there are objects impersonating them as well, as with the gullible bee fooled by the floral pattern on a Persian rug in the poem on page 87. Then there is the strong sense of seasonal change, of the falling of the leaves or the snow, or of the enveloping fog—a constant reminder of a fundamental mystery.

The most central personage of all is the wind. Doubtless there are traditions in every culture that relate the imagination directly to the elements, and the idea could easily extend to modern Persian poetry, where poets often inhabit one or another of the four elements. The great nature poet Sohrab Sepehri (1930–80), for example, is by and large a poet of earth and soil. Forugh Farrokhzad (1935–67), the voice best known abroad, who takes in the view outside her window with an eye to the skyline or the space between buildings, strikes us as a poet of air. There is a poem by Farrokhzad, "The Wind Will Carry Us," which opens with a memorably personalized landscape:

Alas, in this small night of mine
the wind keeps its appointment with the leaves of the trees.
In this small night of mine is the fear of ruin.

Kiarostami, whose use of this poem's title for a recent film suggests his appreciation for it, evokes the wind to a comparable effect. Even though he is unlikely to evince a mood so personally—with an "alas" or with a trope that absorbs the scene into self, as we see in the phrase "this small night of mine"—he, too, is primarily and ultimately a first-person observer who frequently personifies the forces of nature. While Kiarostami rarely expresses or induces feelings of anguish or melancholy, in both poets personal perception works to justify the figurative language as the figurative language defines the poetic voice. In other words, the similarities, though considerable, are thematic, not emotive.

At the same time, in Farrokhzad awareness of the spaces between characters—both the emotional distance and the physical space, the air between images that gives her vignettes their shape—colors the mood of the lyric vision. Kiarostami's sensibility, too, makes us aware of the space between things, the texture of the air, the space in which invisible forces play around us. Yet his is ultimately a more serene and benevolent, perhaps a more ennobling, space. This subtle difference is made concrete in Kiarostami's more rural and less citified variation of Farrokhzad's "air." Nevertheless, his vision, too, is largely philosophical or at least meditative, as distinct from social. In some of these poems, the consciousness contemplating an ordinary scene comes away with the kernel of a thought, distilled from the scene, that seems to stand above it ever so tentatively yet in a genuine philosophical relation to it. Such, for example, is the thought of release that arises from the contemplation of a pair of trembling hands tightly drawing the arrow in the poem on page 38; the momentary hesitation thus concretized leads to a final question: "for the bird . . .?" It is as if the human eye, simply by observing, bestows a meaning on the workings of the world that the mind quickly questions. Conversely, the absence of the human agent is cause not just for regret but for angst. Kiarostami's poems, always placing the human inside the natural, often pointing to hints of a grand design just outside the human reach, share the heritage of Persian mysticism as it is manifested in much modernist poetry, where nature is not only animate but animating.

There is a question that emerges from time to time in the study of the great innovative voices who developed contemporary writing in Persian throughout the twentieth century: did that movement signal a break with tradition or was it a continuation and extension of that tradition? The two translators of this collection have argued on opposite sides of this issue, but we both agree that Kiarostami has developed a unique personal voice capable of synthesizing the two. To say, for instance, that speed is his dominant style is merely to say that Kiarostami has attended to the classical ghazal with its leaps from one image to another, but only to the extent that images and motifs contribute to a coherent mood. The thematics of the Persian ghazal—the parrot in love with sugar, harvests set ablaze, breezes that carry news of the beloved, weeping narcissuses—provide not only a characteristic zigzag motion but a lexicon. While the image of the waxing moon makes sense floating there alone, the reader familiar with Persian may well hear in it a passing echo of the Hafezian ghazal. A close reader of these poems, that is, may see not only the image on the screen but a distinct color in the light passing through the film.

Habitually, nonchalantly, Kiarostami combines the supple lexicon of the Persian language with the vast aesthetic potential of Persian poetry to make that august tradition new. Characteristically, he throws the spotlight on the object of observation rather than on the perceiving mind to keep our attention fixed on the poetic nature of our world. In this way, his poetry embodies and exhibits the most abiding concerns of the entire tradition: the structure of the ineffable, those relations that cannot be reduced to human logic—like the enigma of a dog's fidelity, the bitterness of truth, the puzzle of poverty in the midst of plenty. The poems in this book often acknowledge and celebrate the presence of mystery in our midst. Whether explicitly, such as in the cycle of poems that open with the phrase "the more I think," or more subtly, as in many other instances in the following pages, they place the human within a world of nature, but nature widened to emphasize the mundane and the quotidian as well as the supernatural. Kiarostami has thus grafted the most abiding aspirations of the best of Persian poets, both classical and modern, to contemporary concerns. If he can be said as a filmmaker to have led the art form of the twentieth century to new aesthetic heights, these restless, airy walks with the wind may guide us step by step to a new verbal kinetic.

Walking with the Wind

Poems by Abbas Kiarostami

کرّه اسبی سفید،
از مه می‌آید
و ناپدید می‌شود
در مه.

A white foal
emerges through the fog
and disappears
in the fog.

برف می‌بارد
برف می‌بارد
برف می‌بارد
روز به پایان می‌رسد
برف می‌بارد
شب.

Snow falls
snow falls
snow falls.
The day ends.
Snow falls.
Night.

جاپای عابری در برف
از پی کاری رفته؟
برمی‌گردد؟
از همین راه؟

A passerby's footprints in the snow —
gone on an errand?
Is he coming back?
This way?

گورستان
سراسر
پوشیده از برف.

آب شده
تنها برفِ سه سنگ قبر
هر سه جوان

The graveyard
is covered over
with snow.

Only on three tombstones
is the snow melting —
all three young.

برف‌ها
به سرعت آب می‌شوند
و به زودی پاک می‌شود،
جاپای عابران
از کوچک و بزرگ

The snow
melts so rapidly —
soon those footprints
will be gone,
large and small.

سپیدیِ کبوتر
گم می‌شود در ابرهای سپید،
روز برفی

White of a pigeon
erased in white clouds —
a snowy day.

صدای طبل
هراسان می‌کند
شقایق‌های اطراف جاده را.
آیا باز خواهند گشت؟

The beating of drums
frightens
the roadside poppies.
Will they show themselves again?

صد سربازِ گوش به فرمان
به خوابگاه می‌روند
در آغاز شبی مهتابی

رؤیاهای نافرمان

One hundred obedient soldiers
enter the barracks
early on a moonlit night.

Rebellious dreams!

تکه برفی کوچک
-یادگار زمستانی طولانی-
اوایل بهار...

A little patch of snow —
souvenir of a long winter
in early spring . . .

بنفشه‌های زرد
بنفشه‌های بنفش
با هم
و جدا از هم

Yellow violets
violet violets
together
and apart.

زن سپیدموی
به شکوفه‌های گیلاس می‌نگرد؛
آیا بهار پیری‌ام فرا رسیده است؟

White-haired woman
eyeing the cherry blossoms:
"Has the spring of my old age arrived?"

راهبه‌ی پیر
اندرز می‌دهد
راهبه‌های جوان را
در میان درختان گیلاس

The old nun
dispenses advice
to the young nuns
amid cherry trees.

جوجه‌های یک روزه
تجربه کردند
نخستین باران بهاری را

Day-old chicks
experiencing
their first spring shower.

پروانه به دور خود می‌چرخد
بی‌هدف
در آفتاب ملایم بهاری

Aimlessly
in mild spring sunshine
the butterfly circling round itself.

در بادِ بهاری
ورق می‌خورد دفتر مشق.
کودکی خفته
بر دست‌های کوچک خویش...

In the spring wind
a school notebook's pages turn over —
a child sleeping
on his little hands . . .

راهبه‌ی پیر
صبحانه می‌خورد به تنهایی،
صدای کتریِ جوشان

Whistle of the boiling kettle:
the old nun
is having breakfast alone.

تاج خروس وحشی
بردباری می‌کند
در جمع منظم بنفشه‌های بهاری

The wild cockscomb
bides his time
in the cultivated company of spring pansies.

می‌پرد و می‌نشیند
می‌نشیند و می‌پرد
ملخ
به سمتی که فقط خود می‌داند

It flies and settles
settles and flies away again —
the grasshopper
in the direction it alone knows.

شش راهبه‌ی کوتاه
قدم می‌زنند
میان چنارهای بلند

بانگ کلاغان

Six short nuns
stroll
amid tall sycamores.

The shriek of crows.

یک قطره نور
فرو می‌افتد
از شکافِ آسمان خاکستری
بر اولینَ شکوفه‌ی بهاری

From a crack in the ashen sky
a drop of light
falls
onto the spring's first blossom.

زنبور عسل
مردد می‌ماند
در میان هزاران شکوفه‌ی گیلاس

Amid thousands of cherry blossoms
the honeybee
hesitates.

دستانی لرزان
یک کمان کشیده
لحظه‌ی رهایی
برای پرنده... ؟

Trembling hands,
an arrow drawn tight:
moment of release
for the bird . . .?

رؤیای کشتارِ هزار پرنده‌ی کوچک
بر یک بالش پَر

The dream of a thousand little birds slaughtered
on a downy pillow.

یک سیب سرخ
هزار چرخ می‌زند
در هوا
و می‌افتد
در دست کودکی بازیگوش

A red apple
makes a thousand turns
in the air
and falls
into the hands of a playful child.

در میان صدها
سنگ کوچک و بزرگ
می‌جنبد،
تنها یکی سنگ‌پشت

Among hundreds of rocks
small and large
dawdles
a single turtle.

عنکبوت
کار خود را آغاز کرده است
قبل از طلوع آفتاب

Before sunrise —
the spider
already gone to work.

چشمه‌هایی
در دل کوه‌های دوردست.
کسی آب نمی‌نوشد،
حتا پرنده‌ای

Wellsprings
in the heart of faraway mountains.
Nobody to drink the water,
not even a bird.

چه خوب شد که نمی‌بیند
سنگ‌پشت پیر
پرواز سبک‌بار پرنده‌ی کوچک را

How merciful
that the turtle doesn’t see
the little bird’s effortless flight.

جوانه زد
شکفت
پژمرد
فرو ریخت
حتا یک کس آن را ندید

It sprouted
blossomed
withered
and fell to the ground.
Not a soul to see it.

عنکبوت
دست از کار می‌کشد
لحظه‌ای
به تماشای طلوع خورشید

The spider
stops
and takes a moment's break
to watch the sun rise.

زنبورهای کارگر
کم‌کاری می‌کنند
در نیمروز بهاری

Spring noon:
the worker bees
slow down.

چه آرام
چه باشکوه
بالا می‌آید ماه
از طرف خاوران

How calmly
gloriously
the moon rises
on the eastern horizon.

چگونه می‌تواند زیست
سنگ‌پشت پیر
سیصد سال
بی‌خبر از آسمان

How can
the old turtle live
three hundred years
unaware of the sky?

ستاره‌ی دنباله‌دار
فرو می‌افتد در شبی سیاه
در دل برکه‌ی آرام

صدای آهن گداخته
در آب

One black night
a comet
pierces the pond's heart —

the hiss of hot steel
in the water.

بزرگ شد و بزرگ‌تر
کامل شد
کوچک شد و کوچک‌تر

امشب،
شبی بی ماه

It grew large and still larger.
It grew full
and turned small and smaller.

Tonight
a moonless night.

دریا تاریک
ساحل تاریک
به انتظار خورشید باشم
یا ماه؟

Sea all black
shore black —
should I expect the sun
or the moon?

نور مهتاب
ذوب می‌کند
یخ نازک رود کهن را

Moonlight
thaws
thin ice on the old river.

زنی بیدار
دل‌کنده از نوازش
در کنار مردی خفته

Woman lying awake
beside a sleeping man —
no hope of a caressing hand.

پنج زن آبستن
در سکوت اتاق انتظار
عصر پنج‌شنبه

Five pregnant women
in the silence of the waiting room —
last day before the weekend.

ریواس و شبدر کوهی
گفت و گو می‌کنند، با هم
و گرامی می‌دارند
تابش ملایم آفتاب پاییزی را

The wild rhubarb and the mountain clover
converse
and bask
in the mild sunshine of autumn.

برگ چنار
فرو می‌افتد آرام
و قرار می‌گیرد
بر سایه‌ی خویش
در نیمروز پاییزی

Autumn afternoon:
a sycamore leaf
falls softly
and rests
on its own shadow.

یک قطره باران
می‌غلتد از برگ شمشاد
می‌افتد بر آبی گل‌آلود

A drop of rain
rolls off the box-tree leaf
and falls into the muddy water.

صد درخت تناور
شکست، در باد
از نهالی کوچک
تنها دو برگ
بر باد رفت

A hundred stout trees
have broken in the wind —
from the little sapling
only two leaves
blown away.

با باد بعدی
نوبت کدام برگ است
که فرو افتد؟

As the wind rises
which leaf's turn is it
to fall down?

غازهای وحشی
فرود می‌آیند این بار،
بر نی‌های بریده

This time
the wild geese land
on cut reeds.

زنی آبستن
می‌گرید   بی‌صدا
در بستر مردی خفته

A pregnant woman
weeps silently
in a sleeping man’s bed.

باد
در کهنه را
باز می‌کند
و می‌بندد
با صدا
ده بار

The wind
opens
the old door
and closes it
noisily
ten times.

مردی خسته در راه
تنها
یک فرسنگ
تا مقصد

An exhausted traveler
on his way alone —
one parasang
from his destination.

ماه
به شمشادهای خیس می‌تابد
لحظه‌ای پس از باران

A moment after the rain
the moon
shines on wet box trees.

مهتاب
به درخت کاج می‌تابد
زیر برف سنگین

Moonlight
shines on the pine tree
under heavy snow.

یک گلِ کوچکِ بی‌نام
روییده به تنهایی
در شکاف کوهی عظیم

A little nameless flower
blossoming alone
in the crack of a huge mountain.

صدای رعد
ناتمام می‌گذارد
عوعو سگ را
برفراز ده

The roar of thunder
over the village
interrupts
the dog's bark.

در کوره راه کوهستانی
پیرمرد روستایی در راه
آوای جوانی از دور

An old villager
on the mountain path —
a young man's call from afar.

پل شکسته
سطح آب را می‌خراشد
نور ماه
هرز می‌رود

The sagging bridge
scratches the water's surface
warping
the moonlight.

از دست هیچ کس
کاری ساخته نیست
وقتی آسمان
قصد باریدن دارد

Nobody
can do anything
when the sky
means to shed rain.

سگ سیاه
عوعو می‌کند
برای تازه واردی ناشناس
در شب بی‌ستاره

Starless night:
black dog
barking
at the newcomer.

Spring breeze
steals the hat off the scarecrow's head —
first day of spring . . .

باد بهاری
کلاه از سر مترسک می‌رباید
اولین روز سال نو...

قرص ماه
با احتیاط بالا می‌آید
از قله‌ی آتشفشان

The round moon
rises gingerly
above the volcanic peak.

مه که فرو نشست
قرص خورشید
رنگ پریده
در طرف خاوران

The sun's disk
pale
in the east
as fog settles.

فرو می‌افتد کلید
بی‌صدا
از گردن زنی شالی‌کار
کتری جوشان،
بر اجاق آشپزخانه

The key hanging
from a woman's neck
in a rice paddy
falls off without a sound —
a kettle boils on the kitchen stove.

شصت و شش گام بلند
تا انتهای باغ
با گام‌های راهبه‌ای کوتاه

Sixty-six long steps
to the orchard's other end —
in short nuns' steps.

گاوی آبستن
دو سطل بی‌شیر
در دست مردی در گذرگاه

A pregnant cow —
two empty milk pails
in the hands of a passerby.

قرص نانی
قسمت می‌شود
میان پنج کودک گرسنه

زنی پا به ماه

A loaf of bread
gets distributed
among five hungry boys —

a woman in labor.

زنبورهای کارگر
کار را رها می‌کنند
برای گفت و گویی لذت بخش
در اطراف زنبور ملکه

Worker bees
leave work
for a pleasant chat
around the queen bee.

گاو شیرده
چنان راه می رود
که مرد روستایی در قفا
با دو سطل شیر

The milk cow
walks
just like the villager behind her
with two pails of milk.

زنی پا به ماه
بیدار
در جمع پنج دختر و یک مرد خفته

A woman in labor
awake
surrounded by five girls and a sleeping man.

دو راهبه
سرسنگین
از کنار هم می‌گذرند
میان درختان چنار

Two nuns
heavy-headed
cross paths
among the sycamores.

مهتاب
تابیده از پشت شیشه
بر چهره‌ی مهتابی راهبه‌ی جوان
در خواب

Moonlight
shining through the glass
on the pale face
of the young nun asleep.

آفتاب پاییزی
بر چینه‌ی گلین
مارمولکی هوشیار

Autumn sunshine —
a lizard alert
on the mud-brick wall.

مترسک
عرق می‌ریزد زیرِ کلاه پشمی
در نیمروزِ گرمِ تابستان

At summer noon
the scarecrow
sweats under its woolen hat.

آفتاب پاییزی
از پشت شیشه می‌تابد
بر گُل های قالی
زنبوری خود را به شیشه می‌کوبد

The autumn sun
shines through the window
on the flowers of a carpet.
A bee beats its head against the glass.

میوه های کاج
فرو می‌افتند
یک به یک
از تند باد پاییزی

Pine cones
fall
one by one
in strong autumn winds.

مگس ها
می‌چرخند به دور سر یابوی مرده
هنگام غروب آفتاب

Sunset —
flies circling
around the dead nag's head.

عنکبوت
پیوند می‌زند
این بار
شاخه‌های توت و گیلاس را

This time
the spider
brings together
the branches of the cherry and the mulberry.

بارش باران
بر درختان خشک
آوای زاغی از دور

The pouring rain
on dried-up trees —
from afar the shriek of a crow.

باد
دو نیم می‌کند
تکه ابری کوچک را
برای غرب و شرق
در نیمروز خشکسالی

The wind
slices a little cloud
into two halves:
one for the west, one for the east
at noon on a day of drought.

بچه‌های روستایی
نشانه می‌روند بی‌مهابا
سر حلبین مترسک را

Fearlessly
the village kids target
the scarecrow’s tin head.

مه غلیظ صبحگاهی
بر غوزه‌زار پنبه
صدای رعد از دور

The thick fog of dawn
over a cotton field —
the sound of thunder from afar.

گل‌های آفتابگردان
سرافکنده نجوا می‌کنند
در پنجمین روز ابری

On the fifth day of clouds
sunflowers
whisper with lowered heads.

عنکبوت
با رضایت به حاصل کار خویش می‌نگرد
بین توت و گیلاس

The spider
eyes its handiwork with satisfaction
between the cherry and the mulberry tree.

خورشید می‌تاباند
نخستین انوار طلایی خود را
بر پرده‌ی پرشکوه تار عنکبوت

The sun beams
its first golden rays
on the majestic mantle that is the spider's web.

برف می‌بارد
از ابری سیاه
به سپیدی برف

Snow descends
from the black clouds
with the whiteness of snow.

در زیارتگاه
به هزار چیز اندیشیدم
بیرون که آمدم
برف نشسته بود

Inside the shrine
I thought a thousand thoughts
and when I left
it had snowed.

قاصدک از راه دور
به دیدار برکه آمد
آب از آب تکان نخورد

From far away a dandelion
deigned to settle on the pond
without rippling the water.

عنکبوت
رانده می‌شود
به نرمی
از کلاه راهبه‌ی پیر

Gently
the spider
is shooed away
from the old nun's hat.

گفت و گوی راهبه‌ها
راه به جایی نمی‌برد
سرانجام
وقت خواب است

The nuns' discussion
concludes nothing.
Eventually
it is time to sleep.

برف‌ها
فروریخته می‌شوند از بام
با پارو
چه بی‌مقدار

The snow
shoveled right off the roof
with a snow shovel —
how undignified.

روی طناب رخت
برف پهن کرده‌اند
در این هوای سرد
به این زودی‌ها خشک نخواهد شد
برف

On the clothesline
snowflake linen hangs.
In this cold air
snow doesn't dry up
so fast.

کلاغ سیاه
با حیرت به خود می‌نگرد
در دشت پوشیده از برف

In a snow-covered field
the black-hooded crow
looks at itself dazed.

شب
طولانی
روز
طولانی
عمر
کوتاه

Nights
long
days
long
life
short.

سگ ولگرد
تن می‌شوید
در باران بهاری

The stray dog
washes its body
in spring rain.

راهبه
دست می‌کشد
بر پارچه‌ی ابریشم:
مناسب است برای روپوش؟

The nun
caresses the silk fabric:
would it do
for a gown?

سگ در کمین نشسته
در انتهای کوچه
برای گدای تازه وارد

The dog lies in ambush
at the end of the alley
for the new beggar.

سگ خفته
یک چشم باز می‌کند و می‌بندد
برای دیدن پشه‌ی مزاحم

The sleeping dog
keeps opening an eye and closing it again
to watch the pesky mosquito.

بارش تگرگ
بر تخم گنجشکی خُرد؛
پرواز پرنده‌ای کوچک

Hail lands
on the sparrow's egg —
the flight of a tiny bird.

کبوتر
نخستین شعر حماسی را سرود
هنگام پرواز بر فراز قله‌ی آتشفشان

Flying over a volcanic peak
the dove
composed its first epic song.

باران لاجوردی
بر شکوفه‌های گیلاس
شکوفه‌های رنگین
در غروب بهاری

Azure rain
on cherry blossoms.
Tinted blossoms
at spring sunset.

دوده‌ی شمع
سیاه می‌کند
بالِ رنگینِ پروانه را

Soot from the candle
blackens
the butterfly's colorful wing.

به جوانه نمی‌نشیند
تنها یک درخت
در جمع درختان گیلاس

In the community of cherry trees
one does not blossom
by itself, alone.

As the rain comes down
sunflowers
put their heads together.

گل‌های آفتابگردان
سردرکنار هم
هنگام ریزشِ تندِ باران

مترسک
آبیاری می‌شود
در میان جالیز

The scarecrow
getting irrigated
in the middle of the field.

یکی از راهبه‌ها
چیزی گفت
بقیه خندیدند
با صدای بلند

One of the nuns
said something.
The rest broke
into loud laughter.

دو سنجاقک ماده و نر
از کنار هم می‌گذرند
در میان درختان بلوط

Two dragonflies, one male one female
pass in the air
among the oak trees.

برخورد قهرآمیز دو فاحشه
هنگام خروج از کلیسا
عصر یکشنبه

Angry confrontation between two prostitutes
leaving the church
on Sunday afternoon.

تلی از
تایرهای فرسوده
سگی رنجور
نگهبانی می‌دهد
بی‌مواجب

A heap of
discarded tires:
a decrepit dog
standing watch
free of charge.

زمین لرزه
ویران کرد حتا
انبار غله‌ی مورچگان را

The earthquake
destroyed
even the ants' grain silo.

از هر صد سیب
ده سیب کرمو
برای هر کرم
ده سیب

Out of a hundred apples
ten have worms —
ten apples
to a worm.

سیب کوچک
به دور خود می‌چرخد
از فرو ریختن آبشاری کوچک

The little apple
floats spinning
at the base of a little waterfall.

سگ ولگرد
دم می‌جنباند
برای عابر کور

The stray dog
wags its tail
for the blind passerby.

میوه‌های رنگین
در سکوت سوگواران سیاه‌پوش

Colorful fruits
in the silence of black-clad mourners.

در جمع سوگواران سیاه‌پوش
کودک
خیره به خرمالو می‌نگرد

In the assembly of black-clad mourners
the child
gazes boldly at a persimmon.

گورکن
دست از کار می‌کشد
برای خوردن لقمه‌ای
نان و پنیر

The grave digger
stops work
to take a bite
of bread and cheese.

حاصل دو روز
کار عنکبوت
ویران می‌شود
با جاروی خدمتکار پیر

The spider's harvest
of two days
is left in ruins
by the old housekeeper's broom.

آغاز می‌کند
عنکبوت
این بار
کار تنیدن را
بر پرده‌ای ابریشمین

This time
the spider
begins
to weave
on the silk drape.

ماه می‌شکند
در قاب پنجره

صدای گریه‌ی کودکی نوزاد

The moon breaks
against the window frame —

sound of a newborn crying.

چند کودک دبستانی
گوش سپرده‌اند
بر خط آهنی متروک

A few schoolchildren
have put their ears
on the deserted train track.

مترسکی تنها
در زمینی بی‌خوشه
اوایل زمستان

A lone scarecrow
in an idle field
as winter sets in.

پرندگان
بازی می‌کنند
روی دست و صورت مترسک

کار به آخر رسیده است

Birds
are playing
on the scarecrow's hands and face.

Work must be over.

دو دفتر صد برگ
یک مداد نوک تیز
کوله‌باری اندرز
کودکی در راه

Two hundred-sheet notebooks
one sharpened pencil
one backpack full of advice —
a child well on his way.

کودک دبستانی
راه می‌رود بر ریل کهنه
و تقلید می‌کند ناشیانه
صدای قطار را

The schoolchild
walks on the old rail
clumsily mimicking
the sound of the train.

باد
به رقص وا می‌دارد
خرقه‌ی ژنده‌ی مترسک را
اولین روز سال نو

The wind
moves the scarecrow's tattered robe
to dance —
first day of the new year.

زیر کورسوی چراغ نگهبانی
کودک
نقاشی می‌کشد

پدر در خواب

In the dim light of the switchman's lamp
the child
is drawing

while the father sleeps.

کودک تب دار
نگاه می‌کند از پشت شیشه
با حسرت
بر آدمک برفی

The child with a fever
looks longingly
through the windowpane
at the snowman.

کودک
رفتاری مهربان دارد
با عروسک
مادر... نه چندان

The child
on her best behavior
with the doll.
The mother, well . . .

یک قطره باران
سُر می‌خورد بر روی شیشه
دست کوچک جوهری
پاک می‌کند بخار را
از روی شیشه

A drop of rain
slides over the windowpane.
A little ink-stained hand
wipes the dew
off the window's face.

صدها گردوی تازه
در اطراف کودکی خُرد
با دستان کوچک و سیاه

Hundreds of fresh walnuts
around a small child
with little stained hands.

در معبدی متعلق به
هزار و سیصد سال پیش
ساعت
هفت دقیقه به هفت

In a temple
one thousand three hundred years old
the clock
reads seven minutes to seven.

ساعت مچی
از کار می‌افتد
روی دست مرد نابینا

The watch
on the blind man's wrist
has stopped.

مرد نابینا
ساعت می‌پرسد
از کودک دبستانی

The blind man
asks the schoolchild
for the time.

روستایی
به زمین خود بازمی‌گردد
برای کشتِ بهاری
بدون نیم نَگاهی به مترسک

The villager
returns to his land
for spring seeding —
not even a half-glance at the scarecrow.

کارگران زغال‌سنگ
هیچ کدام ندیدند
بارش نخستین برف زمستانی را

Coal miners:
not one has seen
the first winter snow.

ریزش معدن زغال‌سنگ
پرواز صدها پروانه‌ی سفید

Collapse of the coal mine —
flight of hundreds of white butterflies.

سپیدی برف
چشم کارگران زغال‌سنگ را زد
هنگام خروج از معدن

The snow's whiteness
strikes the eyes of the coal miners
emerging from the mine.

خوب که فکر می‌کنم
نمی‌فهمم
دلیل این همه سپیدی برف را

The more I think
the less I understand
the reason for all the whiteness of the snow.

راهبه‌ها
به توافق نمی‌رسند
سرانجام
بر سر رنگ اتاق غذاخوری

In the end
the nuns
could not agree
on the color of their dining room.

خوب که فکر می‌کنم
نمی‌فهمم
دلیل این همه
نظم و شکوه را
در کار عنکبوت

The more I think
the less I understand
the reason
for all this order and majesty
in the spider's work.

خوب که فکر می‌کنم
نمی‌فهمم
دلیل این همه مهر مادران را
به فرزندان

The more I think
the less I understand
the reason for a mother's love
for her children.

خوب که فکر می‌کنم
نمی‌فهمم
دلیل این همه وفاداری سگ را

The more I think
the less I understand
the reason for the dog to be so faithful.

خوب که فکر می‌کنم
نمی‌فهمم
دلیل پینه‌ی دستانِ تهی‌دستان را

The more I think
the less I understand the reason
for calluses on the hands of the empty handed.

خوب که فکر می‌کنم
نمی‌فهمم
دلیل تلخی حقیقت را

The more I think
the less I understand
why the truth should be so bitter.

The more I think
the less I understand
why the Milky Way
is so distant.

خوب که فکر می‌کنم
نمی‌فهمم
دلیل این همه
بلندی کهکشان را

خوب که فکر می‌کنم
نمی‌فهمم
دلیل این همه
ترس ازمرگ را

The more I think
the less I understand
the reason
to fear death so much.

آیا گوش‌هایم خواهد شنید باز
صدای طغیان رودخانه‌ی مجاور را
هنگام آب شدن برف‌ها؟

Will my ears ever hear again
the sound of the nearby river's rebellious tide
as the snows thaw?

آخرین برگی که به شاخه چسبیده
به خود نوید می‌دهد
تماشای جوانه‌های بهاری را

The last leaf stuck to the branch
clings to the promise
of glimpsing spring buds.

از خواب که پریدم
درست اول بهار بود
نه کم
و نه بیش

When I started up out of sleep
it was just the beginning of spring
no more
no less.

خط کشیده است جت
بر آسمانِ آبی
در اولین روز سال نو

The jet has sketched a line
across the blue sky
on the first day of the new year.

زنبور عسل
مدهوش می‌شود
از عطرِ گلی ناشناخته

The honeybee
is amazed
by the fragrance of an unknown flower.

باران بهاری
پُر آب می‌کند
لانه‌ی کبوتر را

کبوتر به تماشای بهار رفته است

Spring rain
fills the pigeon's nest
with water.

The pigeon is out watching the spring.

پرستوها
امسال باز نمی‌گردند
به جای نخستین؟

Won't the swallows
ever come back
this year?

مار
می‌پیماید عرض خیابان را
بی نگاهی به چپ و راست

The snake
crosses the street
without a glance to left or right.

قطار زوزه می‌کشد
و می‌ایستد

پروانه‌ای خفته بر ریل آهن

The train shrieks
and comes to a halt.

A butterfly sleeps on the rail.

گریه‌ی کودک را
آواز پرنده همراهی می‌کند
تا رسیدن مادر

The cry of the child —
a bird song accompanies it
until the mother returns.

هلال ماهِ یک شبه
مراقبت می‌شود
با تکه ابر پنبه‌ای

A crescent moon of the first night
is being pampered
by a cottony piece of cloud.

خیش زمین را می‌شکافد
و هیچ نمی‌داند گاو
دلیل دردِ دست و پایش را

The plowshare digs the earth
and the ox has no idea
what caused the pain in his limbs.

در نسیم بهار
پرواز چند برگ خشک پاییزی

The scattering of a few withered autumn leaves
in the spring breeze.

وقتی قرص ماه بالا می‌آید
از خاوران
احساس عاشقانه‌ام اوج می‌گیرد
اندکی

As the moon's disk rises
in the east
my feelings of love
wax just a little.

کفش‌هایم خیس می‌شوند
هنگام عبور
از کشت‌زار شبدر

My shoes get soaked
as I cross
the clover field.

خوشه‌های گندم
به خود می‌پیچند
از تندباد بهاری

Sheaves of wheat
twist
in the spring thunderstorm.

صدای زوزه‌ی شغال ماده را
سگ پاسخ می‌دهد
از راه دور
در شبی مهتاب

A dog responds
from afar
to a she-jackal's howls
in the moonlit night.

آینه می‌شکند
در دست زنی نازیبا
صد چشمه روان می‌شود
در دل شبی سیاه

The mirror breaks
in a plain woman's hand —
a hundred streams welling up
in the dead of a dark night.

سایه‌ام
با من همراهی می‌کند
در شب مهتاب

My shadow
keeps me company
this moonlit evening.

وقتی خورشید بالا می‌آید،
از خاوران
احساس عاشقانه‌ام
کاسته می‌شود
اندکی

As the sun rises
in the east
my feelings of love
wane
just a little.

چراغ برمی‌افروزد
در شب توفانی
اصرار عاشق
راه به جایی نمی‌برد

The lamp stays lit
in the night of storm.
The lover's pleas
come to naught.

جوانه‌ی کوچک
فریاد می زند خود را
از میانِ غلافِ سختِ چوبِ گیلاس

The little bud
announces itself loudly
from inside its hard sheath of cherry wood.

گل شیپوری
پُر می‌شود
از باران بهاری

The bowl of the bignonia
fills up
with spring rain.

باران بهاری
فرو می‌ریزد با شتاب
بر بشقاب‌های چرب.
نودختری
خشک می‌کند دستانش را
با دامنی پر گُل

Spring rain
pours in a rush
onto dirty dishes.
A young girl
dries her hands
with her floral skirt.

شبدرها پنهان کرده‌اند در خود
شبنم‌های صبحگاهی را

Within their folds, the clover buds have hidden
many morning dewdrops.

هیچ کس نمی‌داند
جویبار کوچکی
که جاری می‌شود از دل چشمه‌ای خُرد
قصد دریا دارد

Nobody knows
that the little stream
gushing from the heart of a small fountain
is headed for the sea.

بلبلِ آوازخوان
رانده می‌شود
از فریاد مردی خواب‌آلود
در سپیده‌دم بهاری

The singing nightingale
is driven away
by the shrill cry of a man half asleep
at spring dawn.

شیشه‌ی نوشابه شکسته
لبریز
از باران بهاری

The broken soda-pop bottle
fills up
with spring rain.

اسب سم می‌کوبد
بر گلی ناشناس
در جمع هزاران گل و گیاه

The horse stamps his hoof
on an unknown flower
among thousands of flowers and weeds.

باران بر علوفه‌ی خشک
به مشام گاو شیرده می‌رساند
بوی بهار را

The rain on dried fodder
brings the scent of spring
to the milk cow's nostrils.

یابوی بارکش
پا سست می‌کند
هنگام عبور
از کشت‌زار شبدر

The fully loaded nag
slows down
as it passes
by the clover field.

گاو شیرده ماغ می‌کشد
و می‌پراند خواب را
از چشمان مرد خسته
در بعدازظهر تابستان

The milk cow moos
and shoos sleep away
from the weary laborer's eyes
in the summer afternoon.

باد زوزه می‌کشد
در کوچه‌های بی‌تردد
نه عابری
نه سگی حتا

The wind howls
in deserted alleys —
not a passerby,
not even a single dog.

هلال نازک ماه
می افشاند نور اندک خود را
بر صدها داس خسته
در یک شب تابستان

The slender crescent
scatters its pale light
on hundreds of worn-out sickles
on a midsummer night.

انتهای جاده‌ی خاکی
به آسمان ابری می‌رسد
چند قطره باران
بر خاک

The far end of the unpaved road
merges with the cloudy sky —
a few raindrops
in the dust.

تمامی محصول یک سال
یک روزه جمع می‌شود
بر گرده‌ی چارپایی رنجور
روستایی خسته

A whole year's harvest
is gathered in one day
and loaded on the back of a tottering beast
in a tired village.

ابر تیره
به استقبال قرص ماه می رود
در شب مهتابی

The dark cloud
moves forth to welcome the moon's disk
on a moonlit night.

سنبله‌های نورس
سر در آغوش هم.
از ترس باد
یا داس؟

Ripening stalks
in each other's arms —
is it the wind they fear
or the sickle?

داس خسته
به دیوار انبار تاریک
آویخته می‌شود
برای مدتی طولانی

The tired sickle
hangs on the wall
of a dark storehouse
for a long rest.

شش صندلیِ بامبو
با هم مرور می‌کنند
خاطره‌ی آخرین تندباد پاییزی را
در دشت خیزران

Gathered together
in a field of rattan
six bamboo chairs review
the memory of the last autumnal storm.

بید مجنون
سرو بلند
همسایه‌ای غمگین
غروب خزانی

Weeping willow,
towering cypress,
a dejected neighbor —
autumn sunset.

نخستین پاییزِ تنهایی
آسمانی بی ماه
و صد رشته آواز
در دل

The first autumn of solitude,
a moonless sky,
a hundred strands of song
in the heart.

زاغ تشنه
منقار می‌مالد بر خاک
ابری در راه

The thirsty raven
rubs its beak in the dust —
a cloud on its way.

چشمان کلاغ تشنه
به خرمن دور ماه
غروب تابستان

The eyes of the thirsty crow
fixed on the moon's distant harvest —
summer sunset.

باد
قاصدک را بالا می‌برد
تا ارتفاع کاج
لانه‌ی کبوتری ویران از باد

The wind
lifts the dandelion ball
to the height of a pine tree —
a pigeon's nest, dismantled by the wind.

باران بر دریا می‌بارد
کشت‌زاری خشک

Rain falling on the sea —
the fields parched.

هلال ماه نو
سریع‌تر می‌پیماید
گستره‌ی آسمان را
در تندباد زمستانی

The new crescent moon
travels the sky's expanse faster
on the wings
of a winter storm.

هزار کودک عریان
در برف.

کابوس شب زمستانی

A thousand naked children
in the snow.

Midwinter nightmare.

تندبادی که از شرق می‌وزد
تند می‌کند
پرواز کلاغان را
به سوی غرب

A blast sweeping from the east
speeds along
the ravens' flight
westward.

ماهی‌های قزل‌آلا
نمی‌دانند مقصد رودخانه را
و همراه آن می‌روند
تا آب شور

The trout
have no idea where the river leads them —
they accompany it
to salty waters.

شامگاهان
ماهی کوچک
جامانده از تور ماهیگیران
بر ساحل

By night
the little fish wiggles out
of the fishermen's net
onto the shore.

باد
زوزه می‌کشد
گرگ
زوزه می‌کشد
ماه
نهان می‌شود
در پس ابری تیره

Wind
roaring
wolf
roaring —
moon
hides
behind a dark cloud.

به چشم ماه
اینان که امروز می‌نگرندش
هم آنند
که هزاران سال پیش؟

The question in the moon's eye:
are those who watch her today
the same ones
who watched her thousands of years ago?

پل عظیم
مانع می‌شود لحظه‌ای
تابش نور ماه را
بر رود سیم‌گون

For a moment
the great bridge
stops the moonlight
from shining on the silver river.

روستاییِ رنجور
پا به پا همراه چارپایی مجروح
با باری از غوزه‌های پنبه

The limping villager
in step with a wounded beast
under its bulging load of cotton bolls.

ترانه های شالی‌کاران
شاد و غمگین
آهنگ هردو
یکسان

Songs of the rice farmers:
some happy, some sad
their melodies
exactly alike.

در زیارتگاه
به هزار چیز اندیشیدم
بیرون که آمدم
یکی در خاطرم نماند

Inside the shrine
I thought a thousand thoughts.
When I stepped outside
not one was left in my mind.

گفت
از دست من کاری برنمی‌آید
کاش گفته بود
از دلم

She said:
"I just can't."
I wish she had said:
"My heart won't let me."

کرم رها می‌کند
سیب کرم‌خورده را
برای سیبی تازه

The worm exits
the worm-eaten apple
for a fresh one.

قرص ماه
نور می‌افشاند بی‌دریغ
بر کرم شب تاب

The moon's disk
shines its light unconditionally
on the glowworm.

کرم شب تاب
نور می‌افشاند بی‌دریغ
در شب بی ماه

The glowworm
shines its light unconditionally
on the moonless night.

در بازی‌های کودک و مادربزرگ
آن که همیشه می‌بازد
مادربزرگ است

In games between the child and her grandmother
the grandmother
keeps losing.

کودک
درون گهواره
ابعاد تخت خود را نمی‌شناسد
در اتاق سه در چهار

The child
inside a crib
in a three-by-four room
does not know the dimensions of the bed.

گام برمی‌دارم
بر امواج زرد و سرخ
در غروب پاییزی

I stroll
at autumn sunset
along gold and reddish waves.

به هیچ چیز
آن قدر اطمینان ندارم
که به پایان شب
و روز هم

I don't trust anything
as much as the end
of the night
and of the day.

اکنون کجاست؟
چه می‌کند؟
کسی که فراموشش کرده‌ام.

Where is he now,
doing what,
the one I have forgotten already?

همراه باد آمده‌ام
در نخستین روز تابستان
باد مرا با خود خواهد برد
در آخرین روز پاییز

I have come, along with the wind,
on the first day of summer.
The wind will carry me along
on the last day of the fall.

می‌آیم به تنهایی
می‌نوشم به تنهایی
می‌خندم به تنهایی
می‌گریم به تنهایی
می‌روم به تنهایی

I arrive alone
I drink alone
I laugh alone
I cry alone
I'm leaving alone.

نه خاور
نه باختر
نه شمال
نه جنوب
همین جا که من ایستاده‌ام

Not east
not west
not north
not south
only this spot I am standing on now.

فریاد می‌کشم
بر فراز دره‌ای عمیق
در انتظار پژواک

I cry out
across a deep valley
expecting the echo of my voice.

گریه امانم نمی‌دهد
وقتی
جایی برای گریستن نیست

I can’t stop crying
when there’s no room
for crying any more.

همیشه با کسی
قرار ملاقات دارم
که نمی‌آید...
نام او در خاطرم نیست

I always seem to have an appointment
with someone
who will not come . . .
can’t remember the name.

سال‌هاست
مثل پر کاه
در میان فصول
سرگردانم

For years now
I have been suspended
between the seasons
like a blade of straw.

شش کرت جالیز را می‌گذرم
در شب مهتاب
پا در گل می‌گذارم
تا غوزک

I cross a six-furlong field
on the moonlit night —
my feet sink into the mud
up to my ankles.

به دنبال سراب
به آب رسیدم
بی احساس تشنگی

Following the mirage
here I am at the water's edge
without the feeling of thirst.

یک عمر را پشت سر می‌گذارم
در یک لحظه
بر خویشتن می‌گریم

I leave behind a whole lifetime
in a single moment
and I cry for myself.

از صد عابر
یکی می‌ایستد
مقابل بساط من

Out of a hundred passersby
one stops
in front of my stall.

همیشه ناتمام می‌ماند
حرف‌های من
با خودم...

My words
to myself
never seem quite finished . . .

ببخشید و فراموش کنید
گناهانم را
اما نه آن گونه
که به‌کلی فراموش‌شان کنم

Forgive my sins.
Forget them —
but not so much
that I forget them completely.

VOICES AND VISIONS IN FILM

Series Editor
Bruce Jenkins,
Harvard Film Archive

Designer
Lorraine Ferguson

Cover photos
Abbas Kiarostami
Courtesy Andrea Rosen Gallery and Olivier Renaud-Clement
Front: Untitled (#90), 2000
Back: Untitled (#59), 2000

Printing
Eurasia Press, Singapore

Library of Congress Cataloging-in-Publication Data

Kiarostami, Abbas.
[Hamrah ba bad. English & Persian]
Walking with the wind / poems by Abbas Kiarostami ; translated by Ahmad Karimi-Hakkak and Michael Beard.
p. cm.—(Voices and visions in film)
ISBN 0-674-00844-8
I. Karimi-Hakkak, Ahmad. II. Beard, Michael, 1944- III. Title. IV. Series.

PK6561.K52 H3613 2001
892.7'17—dc21

2001039591